Motivation at Work

Motivation at Work

JANE R. MISKELL
VINCENT MISKELL

The Business Skills Express Series

BUSINESS ONE IRWIN/MIRROR PRESS
Burr Ridge, Illinois
New York, New York
Boston, Massachusetts

© RICHARD D. IRWIN, INC., 1994

Mirror Press: David R. Helmstadter
Carla F. Tishler

Editor-in-Chief: Jeffrey A. Krames
Project editor: Stephanie M. Britt
Production manager: Diane Palmer
Designer: Jeanne M. Rivera
Art coordinator: Heather Burbridge
Illustrator: Boston Graphics, Inc.
Compositor: Alexander Graphics
Typeface: 12/14 Criterion
Printer: Malloy Lithographing, Inc.

Library of Congress Cataloging-in-Publication Data

Miskell, Jane R.
    Motivation at work / Jane R. Miskell, Vincent Miskell.
        p.   cm.—(Business skills express)
    ISBN 1-55623-868-1
    1. Employee motivation.   I. Miskell, Vincent.   II. Title.   III. Series.
    HF5549.5.M63M566   1994
    658.3'14—dc20   93–18112
                                                                                      Rev.

Printed in the United States of America
1 2 3 4 5 6 7 8 9 0 ML 0 9 8 7 6 5 4 3

PREFACE

The main challenge for business organizations is keeping employees highly motivated and tuned into the company's goals. When managers try to impose formal or almost military standards on their workers in order to maintain productivity, they may end up provoking rebellious or hostile reactions. The harder the managers push, the less gets done. And even hardworking staff members can fall into slumps that affect the productivity of an entire department.

This book presents practical techniques, strategies, and exercises for managers and supervisors to use in helping unmotivated employees become productive, conscientious, loyal, and dedicated to the goals of their group and company.

Managers are taught first to identify the strengths and weaknesses of staff members, then how to boost morale and increase and maintain productivity by using the motivational strategies presented. This book also provides training for troubleshooting and dealing with employee response to company changes.

Stop being the boss and become a motivator instead!

Jane R. Miskell
Vincent Miskell

ABOUT THE AUTHORS

Jane R. Miskell is an educator and consultant specializing in motivation techniques, stress management, diversity awareness, study skills, and curriculum development. Her clients and affiliations include the United States Navy, California State Prison, Camarillo State Youth Authority, Ventura College, the New School for Social Research, Sterling Associates, and North American Training, Inc. Ms. Miskell is currently the Associate Dean for Student Affairs for Technical Career Institutes in New York.

Vincent Miskell is an educator and trainer in the New York area. Drawing on his professional experience as a supervisor and instructor, Mr. Miskell has formulated an approach to dealing with anxiety in the workplace and implements this approach in training seminars and workshops. He is currently Coordinator of Academic Administration at Technical Career Institutes in New York.

ABOUT BUSINESS ONE IRWIN

Business One Irwin is the nation's premier publisher of business books. As a Times Mirror company, we work closely with Times Mirror training organizations including Zenger-Miller, Inc., Learning International, Inc., and Kaset International, to serve the training needs of business and industry.

About the Business Skills Express Series

This expanding series of authoritative, concise, and fast-paced books delivers high quality training on key business topics at a remarkably affordable cost. The series will help managers, supervisors, and front line personnel in organizations of all sizes and types hone their business skills while enhancing job performance and career satisfaction.

Business Skills Express books are ideal for employee seminars, independent self-study, on-the-job training, and classroom-based instruction. Express books are also convenient-to-use references at work.

CONTENTS

Self-Assessment

Before evaluating the motivational level of your staff, it's helpful to get a reading on your own level of motivation at work. Next to each of the 15 statements below, check the column you feel is most accurate. Give yourself one, two, three, or four points depending on which column you marked: one for always, two for usually, three for sometimes, and four for never.

	Always	Usually	Sometimes	Never
1. I wake up wishing I didn't have to go to work.	_____	_____	_____	_____
2. I am uncomfortable in the company of my co-workers.	_____	_____	_____	_____
3. I prefer to eat lunch alone.	_____	_____	_____	_____
4. I resent being given additional responsibilities at work.	_____	_____	_____	_____
5. I watch the clock for lunchtime, departure time.	_____	_____	_____	_____
6. I try to avoid company gatherings.	_____	_____	_____	_____
7. I refuse to discuss my personal life at work.	_____	_____	_____	_____
8. I listen to or engage in gossip at work.	_____	_____	_____	_____
9. I resent it when others get promoted.	_____	_____	_____	_____
10. I feel my salary is too low.	_____	_____	_____	_____
11. I look in the classified section for better job opportunities.	_____	_____	_____	_____
12. I hate to discuss work at home.	_____	_____	_____	_____
13. I have nightmares related to work.	_____	_____	_____	_____
14. I feel insecure about my performance.	_____	_____	_____	_____
15. I feel insecure about my position with my company.	_____	_____	_____	_____

Now add up the points. Total = _____

If you scored between 15 and 30 points, then you have a problem with job satisfaction and motivation.

If you scored between 31 and 50 points, then you are in good company. Many supervisory personnel feel this level of motivation about their work.

If you scored between 51 and 60 points, congratulations! You are well on your way to conveying this high level of motivation to your staff.

1 | Identifying Employee Types

This chapter will help you to:

- Identify seven common mismotivated types of employees.
- Consider individual strategies for motivating each type.
- Evaluate the example you set.
- Classify the mismotivated employees on your staff.

If you could administer the Self-Assessment you just completed to the employees that you supervise (and could expect honest answers), your job as a manager would be infinitely easier. You'd be able to inventory your employees' motivational levels, pinpoint their problems, and gain insight for developing a plan of action.

Most people, however, are rarely so easy to read, so you'll have to identify (through observation) those staff members who need motivation. Since most mismotivated employees fall into general categories, the following examples can help you recognize unmotivated employees and create a plan to motivate them.

The Manager

Douglas arrives at work at 8:30, his usual time. The office is not scheduled to open until 9 A.M., but he likes the quiet time to get organized and plan for the day ahead. As department manager, he is also setting an example for his staff, which had some punctuality problems when he took over the department about six months ago. Punctuality has improved slightly, but several other problems are now emerging.

The Complainer

Jeff hurries in just about 9, disheveled, out of breath, and obviously agitated. He immediately starts complaining about his difficulties with mass transit, crowds, or the weather, traffic, and the economy. He looks at his in-box and loudly states that he seems to have more assignments than the other staff members. Throughout the day, he continues to complain that he is the only one working diligently—although he appears to spend most of his time observing what the other employees are doing.

The Sicklie

Marie regularly calls in five minutes after nine to report weakly that she cannot make it into work due to food poisoning, assorted viruses, horrible colds, migraine headaches, or back pain. These maladies seem to occur right before or after a holiday or weekend.

The Not-My-Jober

Vicky is usually on time and always very cheerful. She sorts through her in-box and promptly delivers to Douglas all those assignments that are "clearly not her job." Whenever Douglas points out that most of the tasks do come within her range of responsibilities, she pleasantly replies that although she disagrees, she'll do them because she wants to keep her job. When Douglas makes any routine request, Vicky mentions another employee who "usually handles that sort of thing."

The Perfectionist

Gina arrives precisely five minutes before 9 every day. She gets to work at exactly nine o'clock and doesn't stop until exactly noon when she promptly leaves for lunch, regardless of her workload or deadlines. If she receives a memo which contains any errors or misinformation, she immediately brings it to the attention of the author. Her reports are so scrupulously prepared that it takes her an inordinate amount of time to produce even the simplest document. Gina gets so involved in details that even simple tasks become mammoth, time-consuming projects.

The Procrastinator

Frank arrives anywhere from five to thirty-five minutes late every day. He stopped making excuses long ago because tardiness is not an issue for him—it's a custom.

He is so charming, pleasant, and entertaining, that when he does arrive, everyone is happy to see him and no one mentions the time. Frank loves people and thrives on interaction with everybody. Few people are able to stay angry with him, although he

1

gives everyone ample reason. He regularly misses appointments, forgets to return calls, and delays every task to the last minute.

Frank never feels pressure because deadlines don't exist for him. His personality remains upbeat, calm, and confident. The manager is constantly frustrated by Frank's procrastination.

The Half-Hearted Employee

Sal arrives for work anywhere from fifteen minutes early to fifteen minutes late. He generally appears totally oblivious to the time. Whenever he's questioned about overdue reports, he never seems sure which report is being requested, but he always answers vaguely that it is almost done. Sal invariably hands in his reports, but they usually need extensive revision. Because even the subjects of Sal's reports are vague, it is difficult to determine his actual findings. Sometimes his familiarity with the subject matter is in doubt.

The Angry Underminer

Leon arrives at 9 A.M. and greets the entire staff in a friendly manner. He chats briefly with everyone but leaves Douglas for last. When he passes Douglas's office he simply says, "Good morning," as if it takes some great effort. Leon will do anything asked of him but is sure to mention to the others that he has yet another new task that he has no choice but to accept. Douglas feels tension whenever he encounters Leon chatting with others because it is clear that they are talking about him in a negative way. It is no secret that Leon interviewed for the department manager job six months ago and became bitter when Douglas got the job instead. ■

Suggestion

Power Breakfasts

Schedule an early breakfast meeting with the staff and provide a simple breakfast for the entire staff. Arrange for a brief meeting to follow. If the meeting is mandatory and scheduled for an early hour, employees must make an effort to be there on time—it should set a precedent for those with punctuality problems. The meeting agenda needs to be short because this really is an opportunity for the staff to gather in a positive, congenial atmosphere.

WHO ARE THESE PEOPLE?

Once managers have identified the particular mismotivated types within their department, individual strategies can be planned and implemented. For some, it may take less than a week to improve the symptoms of mismotivation. For others, it may take months and some extraordinary efforts to redirect a mismotivated staff.

Regardless of what type an employee is, each one will appreciate the efforts of the manager to work out problems rather than simply initiate progressive discipline leading to the loss of a job.

INSIGHT AND ACTION

Jeff, the only open complainer in the group, is a strong negative force. He voices complaints about issues that most people learn to accept, such as poor mass transit, heavy traffic, the gloomy economic picture, and various weather problems. These issues are beyond the average person's control. When constantly verbalized, complaints like these drain energy, make people feel helpless, and dull the sharp focus needed to be productive on the job.

As a manager, Douglas needs to combat this negative energy drain. Douglas might try initiating a discussion about the work location. The ensuing discussion should include everyone. In a relaxed and open discussion, people may mention the horrors that they experienced in other locations. Douglas has helped everyone to acknowledge that there are better as well as worse places to work, and that some negative aspects of working are common to all job locations.

This might lead to a general problem-solving session in which all members of this group share solutions about the best way to focus on the positive aspects of having a stable job.

With Marie, Douglas should schedule a private meeting to discuss attendance. Douglas must make an effort to focus on Marie's health, rather than the department's productivity. He might even recommend a good internist or suggest a short leave of absence for testing to determine the cause of her frequent illnesses. Citing the number of days that she has been out in the last six months should make Marie realize the extent of her absenteeism. She may be surprised when confronted with the exact number of missed work days.

Douglas must remain sympathetic, in case the absences are a result of legitimate illnesses. However, Marie may be exaggerating her maladies to avoid work responsibilities. A sympathetic discussion will serve as a warning that her absenteeism is noticeable and problematic. If the absences persist without documented medical cause, Douglas may need to send a memo to Marie warning her that her job is in jeopardy.

When Vicky goes through her ritual of sorting out unwanted assignments, Douglas must employ a preemptive strike. He should leave only those assignments that he knows she will accept. The ones she'll probably reject should be hand-delivered by Douglas himself. He can present each new assignment with: "I know this assignment is slightly out of the ordinary, but your work in this area is very well done and I would like to give you an opportunity to expand your work load to include this related area." If she responds by saying that she has no time, Douglas could show concern and then tell her he is confident that she will be able to manage her time effectively—but to keep him informed about the extra time needed to accomplish her tasks. If she continues to balk, he should encourage her to give it a try because she is the best one for the job. He may need to follow up with a discussion of priorities.

Gina is a perfectionist at work, and is probably a perfectionist in many other aspects of her life. Douglas will not be able to change her fundamental style. However, he must try to modify some of these habits at work with reminders about the priority of content and productivity over format. He should also remind her that timeliness is just as important as delivering a polished product. Douglas must explain that delay, for the sake of perfection, tends to dim the insights her work initially showed.

Frank, however, is a nonperfectionist procrastinator. Frank needs specific deadlines, as well as frequent checks, to determine how far along he has gotten with his assignments. Douglas needs to give Frank advice that almost contradicts what he told Gina. Frank must learn to tighten up his structure and organization, and stay within the boundaries of his job. Although Frank is popular with his co-workers he needs to learn the rules of the workplace and increase his productivity in order to remain a valued employee.

Sal fears commitment. He does not want to be controversial and wants everyone's approval. If he states his opinions too strongly, he fears that he risks disagreement, disapproval, and disciplinary action. Douglas can encourage him to commit to a strong opinion in a report or in a conversation by agreeing with Sal or by saying, "I see your point and it's a good one." Sal will probably never be considered opinionated, but at least he can be encouraged to make clearer statements in his reports. By encouraging Sal to feel safe about voicing his opinions, Douglas may be able to get Sal into the commitment habit.

Leon is in the negative habit of undermining Douglas's efforts and demoralizing the staff. Dealing with Leon will be very tricky because Leon's divisiveness may be difficult to counteract. Douglas may not be able to reestablish his leadership. It is critical that Douglas establish his authority through frequent formal and informal meetings with Leon and all the employees to discuss projects, assignments, or problems. He should use these opportunities to establish trust and to diminish the influence of this rival.

Douglas could openly address the issue of low morale and negative energy at a formal meeting. Although this could offer Leon an opportunity to challenge Douglas and establish his own leadership, a meeting provides a greater opportunity for Douglas to deliver a positive, strong, supportive message to the staff—while deflecting Leon's negative intentions. Douglas can reassure the staff that as the legitimate leader of the department he has their best interests in mind while remaining calm, confident, and in control.

■ Review & Practice

What kind of an example are you setting for your staff?

_____

1. Are you punctual?

   Always   Sometimes   Almost never

2. How many sick, vacation, and/or personal days have you taken this year?

   0 to 10   11 to 20   More than 20

3. How often are you late at meeting deadlines?

   Always   Sometimes   Almost never

4. Do you greet each employee as he/she arrives?

   Always   Sometimes   Almost never

5. Do you evenly distribute job assignments?

   Always   Sometimes   Almost never

6. Are you willing to pitch in and assist an employee who is having difficulty with a particular task?

   Always   Sometimes   Almost never

7. Do you complain about other managers, directors, or supervisors in front of your staff?

   Always   Sometimes   Almost never

8. Do you promptly respond to requests from your staff?

   Always   Sometimes   Almost never

_____

Identify the mismotivated employees on your staff and detail any attempts you have made to correct the problems.

_____

1. Complainers_____

   _____

   _____

2. Sicklies_____

   _____

   _____

3. Not-My-Jobers

4. Perfectionists

5. Procrastinators

6. Half-Hearted Employees

7. Angry Underminers

Chapter Checkpoints

✓ Be sympathetic and supportive.

✓ Don't ignore problems.

✓ Schedule frequent, brief meetings.

✓ Encourage participation and discussion at the meetings.

✓ Remain calm, confident, and in control.

✓ Be flexible and fair.

✓ Plan individual strategies for mismotivated types.

✓ Set a good example.

2 | The Causes of Dissatisfaction

This chapter will help you to:

- Recognize and handle employee dissatisfaction.
- Separate external influences on job dissatisfaction from personal concerns.
- Learn to share employees' concern over external influences.
- Build trust by responding to employees' dissatisfaction in a conciliatory, sincere, and sympathetic manner.

Before you focus on causes for individual dissatisfaction, take the broader picture into consideration. Employees may be unmotivated and unproductive because of issues not immediately related to their jobs:

Geographical location of company.

State of the national economy.

State of the local economy.

Age of the company.

Climate of the area.

Size of the company.

Company management style.

All or some of these factors may have a significant influence on the level of motivation within a business.

LOCATION, LOCATION, LOCATION

For people working in a large city, stress is a daily reality. Many city-dwellers have been conditioned to accept the hazards of city life, but an underlying feeling of distress and tension may be the result. This can be an unconscious cause of job dissatisfaction.

2

CLIMATE CONTROL

How do you feel on a dreary, cold morning? How does a steamy, humid day affect you? How would you describe your mood on a bright, sunny day? If you live in an area where the weather conditions are extreme, then you know how the mood of the general populace can be affected. Although no one can control or change weather patterns, managers may need to be sensitive to changes in mood related to the weather.

2

ECONOMIC EFFECTS

The economy is a source of much speculation, prediction, and discussion, and is a concern for most people. Many employees are fearful, insecure, or fatalistic. Not only is the competition for existing jobs fierce, people may feel pressure because so many qualified applicants want their jobs.

It is vital that employees feel secure in their positions. Managers should make every effort to make the workers feel confident, secure, and appreciated.

UPSTART OR VETERAN?

New companies sometimes have fewer morale problems because the overall mood is usually optimistic. Many people are excited about the prospect of being involved with a business from the ground floor up. Their role in its success and growth is more integral than it may be for employees in older, established companies.

However, profit sharing, bonus plans, and pension funds in more established companies may be very appealing.

BIGGER THAN A BREADBOX?

The size of a company can determine the effect that cut-backs, lay-offs, hiring and wage freezes, and downsizing will have. In large companies, changes may affect only a few employees without lessening overall morale. In small companies, the slightest change may affect every employee and morale will fluctuate drastically with each modification.

STARCH OR NO STARCH IN THE COLLARS?

Management style directly affects the attitudes of employees. Because one-third to one-half of employees' waking hours are spent at work, they must feel comfortable with their companies' work style. Employees whose styles are in direct conflict with the dominant management style of a firm, whether it is large or small, will become a source of irritation to everyone. Whether the dominant management style is formal or casual, relaxed or militaristic, employees need to adapt, or find companies that fit their personal styles.

INSIGHT AND ACTION

Insightful managers are able to separate uncontrollable influences on job dissatisfaction from the purely personal ones in order to create plans to combat dissatisfaction. Let's take another look at the staff of mismotivated employees introduced in Chapter 1. Is their dissatisfaction a result of personal issues, or is it related to problems on a larger scale?

RELOCATION?

Chronic complainers such as Jeff may simply be ducks out of water. Jeff does not seem able to adapt to the stress of a big city. He probably would be more comfortable in a small town where traffic, crowds, and mass transit are not factors in the typical work week. His complaints may simply be expressions of frustration from working in an environment that does not suit him. When Douglas discusses the pros and cons of various job locations, Jeff needs to think about ways to adjust to big-city stress, or to leave.

By allowing himself more travel time in the morning, Jeff could immediately reduce his stress by about 50 percent. Even leaving fifteen minutes earlier would automatically lower the pressure that Jeff feels when his bus or train is delayed by heavy rush hour traffic. Having a good novel to read might also help him to focus on something other than the time.

DOMESTIC DISORDER?

For sicklies like Marie, poor health may reflect troubles at home. Domestic upheavals, such as squabbling among family members, family sickness, change in a spouse's employment, financial difficulties, children in distress, or any other disruption may be what's really making Marie sick. Marie's absenteeism may be a statement that she cannot handle her life.

Douglas should schedule a confidential talk with Marie. She may be relieved to discuss the real cause of her chronic absences. If Douglas suspects that the problem is serious, he should refer Marie to the appropriate agency and urge her to seek counseling.

Douglas needs to express his wholehearted support for Marie. He must discreetly inquire whether or not she has followed up on his suggestion to seek help. Douglas's concern may compel her to take necessary action. He should let her know that she has a limited, although reasonable, amount of time to improve her attendance record. He may even ask her what she considers to be a fair amount of time. This way she will actually be setting her own deadline.

If there is no significant improvement after the time limit elapses, he should suggest a leave of absence during which she will try to settle her domestic situation.

NIT-PICKING

Not-my-jobers and perfectionists, such as Vicky and Gina, may simply be insecure. Vicky is reluctant to do any new job because she fears making errors. By commenting that certain tasks are normally handled by others, she is likely trying to excuse herself because she does not have confidence in her capability to handle a new task.

New assignments represent the risk that she will be criticized, disappoint her supervisor, appear to be incompetent, or that her work will come under scrutiny.

Vicky wants a limited, uncomplicated role in the company. Although she may feel fulfilled and satisfied with limited work, few companies allow employees to completely define their own tasks. She may have grown to resent others for not assuming her responsibilities.

Both Gina and Vicky need to be reassured that they are competent and proficient workers. Douglas must do his best to convince them that minor errors are expected and revisions may only be as a result of a change in information or style, not as a result of shoddy work or carelessness.

FOOTLOOSE AND FANCY-FREE

Half-hearted employees, such as Sal, or procrastinators, such as Frank, may also be unfocused in their private lives. There are some people who drift through life, handling important matters only when they approach red-alert status. They leave the planning up to others and then change plans at the last minute because something better has come along.

Procrastinators like Frank refuse to allow responsibilities, limits, rules, or protocol to ruin their good time. These people seem to be able to always land on their feet and escape the consequences of their irresponsible actions.

2

Half-hearted employees and procrastinators prefer to leave situations as open-ended as possible. They feel most comfortable when work requires the greatest flexibility. If they must complete a task or commit strongly to an idea, they are closing the door on change. When work can be left undone until the last minute, they have more options. Some talented procrastinators and half-hearted employees become masters of improvisation with impressive eleventh-hour solutions. Others may miss deadlines or submit incomplete work.

Douglas must make the most of Frank's positive effect on the staff by encouraging his carefree affability. When dealing with difficult interpersonal problems such as unhappy clients or interdepartmental rifts, Frank should be selected to represent the staff.

For Sal, being noncommittal is much better than being controversial. If Douglas can assign fact-based research reports to Sal, with strict deadlines for a rough draft, a final draft, and a final report, Sal would become accustomed to meeting frequent deadlines. With such a schedule, he'd be able to reserve his judgment to the very last minute.

In the meantime, Douglas is able to make revisions on the earlier drafts of Sal's reports. When Sal hedges, Douglas can insert stronger language that will guide Sal to a clearly expressed conclusion. Over time, Sal will be trained to use more definite language in future reports.

STORM WARNING

Angry underminers create barriers to harmony and productivity no matter where they go. Everyone suffers from the tension they generate because storm clouds seem to hover around them; no one is sure when their lightning will strike. Everyone begins to work around them, since it is so difficult and dangerous to work with them. Leon's hostility stems from professional jealousy.

Sometimes angry underminers don't want a promotion or another's job. They may suddenly decide that a policy change within their department or in their company should be resisted, or they may believe that they are disliked by a supervisor and decide to launch an attack. Unfortunately, their attacks usually spread to other issues and affect everybody's morale.

The specific cause is not as important as quelling the anger as soon as it becomes obvious. Speaking to the employee directly is the first step. If the manager is conciliatory, sincere, and sympathetic to an employee's concerns, the anger may abate. Even if the employee doesn't immediately respond, his co-workers will feel relieved that the manager has taken action and will likely actively support his efforts.

HOW'S THE WEATHER INSIDE?

One important key to becoming a successful motivator is to recognize and deal with employee dissatisfaction. If the causes are beyond anyone's control, *don't ignore the workers' concern—share it*. If the initial attempt doesn't solve the problem, at least the attempt will be appreciated. Managers should display a sincere concern for their employees' well-being. It is a means for building trust and confidence in your leadership.

■ **R e v i e w & P r a c t i c e**

Name three typical problems you must deal with on a daily basis:

1. _____
_____
_____

2. _____
_____
_____

3. _____
_____
_____

Find three positive ways to view the problematic employee behavior covered in this chapter.

Example: Marie called in sick again.

It's not too busy, her attendance isn't critical.
Maybe she will finally be able to resolve her problems.
It's an opportunity to see if the new temp works out.
I may need her if Marie takes a leave of absence.

1. _____
2. _____
3. _____

Chapter Checkpoints

✓ Share workers' concerns—don't ignore them.

✓ Be conciliatory, sincere, and sympathetic.

✓ Build trust and confidence.

3 | Staff Meetings—Let's Make a Deal

This chapter will help you to:

- Handle employee dissatisfaction by making deals in which everybody wins.
- Examine the value of scheduling regular, frequent, and short staff meetings.
- Evaluate your own practices with respect to staff meetings.

Marie arrives at work 40 minutes late. Vicky hands back three assignments that she doesn't consider her responsibility. Jeff is steaming because Gina accused him of misplacing two important client file folders. Although Sal has an important report due tomorrow, he is spending most of his time on personal calls. Frank is surreptitiously playing a video golf game on his computer. Leon is spending most of the morning in another department, supposedly looking for a client's file. Douglas is beginning to lose his patience. ■

TIME OUT

Now is a good time for Douglas, the manager, to leave the office. A short walk outside would give Douglas a chance to regain his patience. A quick analysis of the scenario indicates that none of the problems, individually, are urgent. Douglas should wait until the next staff meeting to address the issues that concern him. He should not single anyone out. It would be better to present the problems initially as occasional rule infractions that everyone is guilty of at one time or another.

3

SELECT A SOLUTION

Marie knows that she is late. She probably appreciates Douglas for not mentioning it at the time. When Douglas addresses the issue of tardiness at the regular staff meeting, he should also mention himself as having been late occasionally. He could suggest that if an employee has a tardiness problem, two solutions should be considered.

The first solution is to change the work schedule to a later start time. Rather than a typical 9 to 5 work schedule, 9:30 to 5:30 or 10 to 6 might be easier for the employee.

The second solution is to make up lost time by staying later. In Marie's case, she should have stayed until 5:40, to compensate for the 40-minute delay in her arrival.

Douglas is displaying flexibility and fairness. He is giving the staff an opportunity to decide for themselves how to solve a problem that affects almost everyone at least once. He is offering them a deal in which everybody wins.

NEW WORK, NOT OVERWORK

Although Vicky is the most vocal about misdelegated work assignments, occasionally most people feel that they are being asked to do someone else's job. However, Douglas should present the work as cross-training. At the regular staff meeting, he should say that sometimes it will be necessary to do work that is normally assigned to someone else. This is a good opportunity to work more closely with others and to expand knowledge of procedures. It is also a break in the monotony of doing the same type of work every day.

This will provide the employees with an incentive to request work in particular areas that they had always been interested in. They will see this as an opportunity for career growth, rather than overwork.

SIBLING RIVALRY?

Jeff and Gina must learn to respect each other's modus operandi. Gina is fussy, fastidious, and obsessive. She gets the job done. Jeff is careless, disorganized, and irresponsible. He gets the job done. Douglas is well aware of his employees' idiosyncrasies but he remains flexible because they are both valuable for their knowledge, skills, and ability to produce whatever is needed.

It annoys Gina that Jeff is so disorganized, so she criticizes him whenever she can. Her judgment of him justifies her own compulsive behavior. She feels that anyone so careless will lose important things and she waits for opportunities to point this out. Two files are missing so it is clear to her that Jeff is the culprit. Though Jeff cannot find the files, he knows they are somewhere in his office and it is just a matter of time before they turn up. He resents being judged by Gina.

3

Douglas should gently admonish both for being so extreme in their organizational habits. He should mention the need for tolerance and compromise.

"HI, ARE YOU BUSY?"

Sal is avoiding his deadlines by socializing on company time. Personal calls are a chronic problem in almost any work environment. Rather than compounding Sal's guilt, Douglas should address this issue in a very general way.

Douglas should personalize the problem by mentioning that his mother called him at work and got him upset about something that could easily have waited for a later time. He should say that because calls affect his mood and productivity at work, he discourages calls from family and friends, and limits those he does receive to less than five minutes.

He could suggest that the staff follow his example and spare themselves the aggravation of being disturbed at work with personal problems. Not only will Sal get the message, others will surely curtail their personal calls.

Another way for Douglas to address this problem is to enter Sal's office while he is talking on the phone. Douglas should say, "When you are off the phone, I need to speak with you about that report that's due soon." If Douglas interrupts every time he sees Sal on calls that are personal and extend more than five or ten minutes, Sal will surely get the hint. If not, Sal must be directly warned that the calls are beginning to interfere with his productivity and they must be limited.

■ **S u g g e s t i o n** ────────────────

Brief is Better

Try to schedule meetings on a weekly basis. More frequent, shorter meetings are much better than monthly, hour-long meetings. Vary the times that the meetings are held. Surprise the staff by occasionally providing refreshments. Try not to have more than five items on the agenda—at least three positive items for every two negative items. Always end the formal presentation with something positive. Allow at least 10 minutes for an open discussion.

WHAT'S THE SCORE?

Frank is escaping from responsibility, routine, and authority by sneaking in a video game during work hours. He knows he shouldn't be doing it, but the enjoyment of playing a game is too tempting for him to resist. Douglas can make a note of the time Frank spends playing and at the end of the week, he can mention the amount of time owed.

However, if all of Frank's work has been handed in and there is no work pending, it might not be necessary to mention any time owed. Douglas could casually inquire about the game that is being played so that Frank knows that he is aware of it. Douglas might ask to borrow the game so that he may try it during his lunch hour—a subtle hint that it's okay to play during free time.

The important thing is not to reinforce childish behavior by assuming the role of a parent. Douglas should not parent Frank, he should manage him.

MISSING IN ACTION

Part of Leon's challenging behavior includes frequent absences from the office. Rather than risk an open confrontation with Leon, Douglas' staff meeting agenda should include a request that employees inform the receptionist of their location, in case there is an important call to be forwarded, or someone is looking for them.

Douglas should mention that interdepartmental visits (another of Leon's habits) are a good way to improve communication and cooperation, but that the visits should be brief, justifiable, and announced. Douglas may seem to be encouraging the absences from the office, but in fact he is trying to manage them. This fact will probably not be lost on Leon or on any of his co-workers.

WANT TO PLAY?

The object of deal-making is to avoid disciplinary action. It is a way of handling departmental problems without singling out one employee. All of these problems are fairly typical and can be dealt with positively if the manager is creative. By offering a compromise, a solution, or a deal, Douglas avoids uncomfortable disciplinary procedures. A manager can gain much goodwill and loyalty by being flexible, fair, and realistic.

3

Motivation Evaluation

Check your ability as a motivator by indicating next to each statement below: 4 points for always, 3 points for sometimes, 2 points for occasionally, and 1 point for never.

_____   **1.** I greet each employee pleasantly.

_____   **2.** I distribute work evenly.

_____   **3.** I listen to employees' problems attentively.

_____   **4.** I solicit opinions and ideas from employees.

_____   **5.** I praise employees for work well done.

_____   **6.** I encourage skill and training development.

_____   **7.** I am successful at resolving employee conflicts.

_____   **8.** I keep everyone informed.

_____   **9.** I involve all employees in decision and policy making.

_____   **10.** I am sensitive to my staff's moods and personality types.

_____   **11.** I encourage my staff to accept new challenges.

_____   **12.** I take time to visit employees in their offices and work stations.

_____   **13.** I offer constructive criticism in private.

_____   **14.** I promptly respond to requests from my staff.

_____   **15.** I see myself as the captain of a spirited team.

Now add up the points. Total = _____

If you scored between 15 and 30 points, it's likely your staff feels uncomfortable and unmotivated.

If you scored between 31 and 50 points, then you are on your way to building a strong, spirited team.

If you scored between 51 and 60 points, you are already a strong team motivator.

◼ R e v i e w   &   P r a c t i c e

1. How often do you schedule staff meetings?

   Daily ____   Weekly ____   Monthly ____   Annually ____

2. How long do the meetings usually last?

   15 to 20 minutes ____   20 to 30 ____   30 to 45 ____   45 to 60 ____
   More than one hour ____

3. How many items are on the typical agenda?

   1 to 5 ____   6 to 10 ____   More than 11 ____

4. How many of the items are disciplinary?

   More than half ____   Less than half ____   None ____

5. How much time is allotted for a group discussion?

   5 to 10 minutes ____   15 to 20 minutes ____   30 minutes ____
   More than 30 minutes ____

3

Chapter Checkpoints

✓ Avoid disciplinary action.

✓ Offer deals in which everybody wins.

✓ Teach employees to tolerate, respect, and compromise with each other.

✓ Improve communication and cooperation between workers and departments.

4 | Creating Camaraderie

This chapter will help you to:

- Identify your psychological type.
- Identify the psychological types of your staff.
- Learn to unite your team.

There are many ways to unite a group of people. The most effective campaigns involve finding a common cause. Issues such as the environment, women's rights, and gun control easily attract devoted groups of supporters. Uniting a work team is more difficult because it is harder to instill a single shared goal or purpose. To create a shared goal you must discover what individual needs must be met in order for members to feel motivated.

Before you analyze the needs of the team players, it is important for you as the manager to identify your own psychological type and your needs and motivators. The following Psychological Type Survey will help analyze these factors.

PSYCHOLOGICAL TYPE SURVEY

Circle (*a*) or (*b*) for each item:

1. Do you tend to be:
   - E   *a.* Talkative even among strangers.
   - I   *b.* Quiet except among friends or relatives.

2. Are you better at:
   - S   *a.* Observing the status quo.
   - N   *b.* Seeing possibilities.

3. Which upsets you more:
- T   *a.* Illogical ideas or actions.
- F   *b.* Human conflicts.

4. Do you usually act:

    J   *a.* According to some plan.

    P   *b.* Spontaneously.

5. When faced with new experiences, do you:

    E   *a.* Usually join right in.

    I   *b.* Hesitate before joining.

6. When are you at your best:

    S   *a.* Working with details.

    N   *b.* Working with overall patterns.

7. When giving bad news, do you tend to be:

    T   *a.* Too blunt.

    F   *b.* Too tactful.

8. Are you more often:

    J   *a.* Too decisive.

    P   *b.* Too indecisive.

9. Do you spend more time on:

    E   *a.* Activities with plenty of action.

    I   *b.* Quiet activities.

10. Are you more interested in:

    S   *a.* Established facts.

    N   *b.* New theories.

11. When judging people, do you tend to:

    T   *a.* Apply the same rules to everyone equally.

    F   *b.* Show some special sympathy for individual circumstances.

12. Is it more comfortable for your plans to be:

    J   *a.* Decided.

    P   *b.* Left open.

4

4

13. At a gathering, a party, or meeting, would you be:

E   *a.* Near the center of activities.

I   *b.* Off to the side with one or two others.

14. You do better in jobs requiring:

S   *a.* Careful checking of facts and figures.

N   *b.* New approaches and inventive ideas.

15. Is your evaluation style:

T   *a.* Abstract, as if you are not involved.

F   *b.* Personal, as if you are always involved.

16. During introductions, do you usually:

E   *a.* Greet people easily.

I   *b.* Feel a little awkward.

17. Are you:

S   *a.* Very practical.

N   *b.* Very imaginative.

18. Is it easier for you:

J   *a.* To meet deadlines.

P   *b.* To adapt to last minute changes.

19. Are you more concerned with:

T   *a.* Ideas that are logical.

F   *b.* People's feelings and harmony.

20. Do you find choice-making:

J   *a.* Easy.

P   *b.* Difficult.

21. What kinds of friendships do you have:

E   *a.* Many close friendships.

I   *b.* Few close friendships.

22. Do you like to solve problems with:

    S   *a.* Standard procedures and routines.

    N   *b.* Novel approaches.

23. Do you generally:

    T   *a.* Need to think how you feel about a person or situation.

    F   *b.* Know without thinking how you feel about a person or situation.

24. Do you live your life:

    J   *a.* According to many plans.

    P   *b.* For the moment.

25. Do you tend to:

    E   *a.* Start talking before thinking.

    I   *b.* Answer carefully only after thinking.

26. Which describes you better:

    S   *a.* Very realistic.

    N   *b.* Very creative.

27. In problem-solving, do you:

    T   *a.* Sometimes forget about other people's feelings.

    F   *b.* Always carefully consider others' feelings.

28. Which term describes you most accurately:

    J   *a.* Organized.

    P   *b.* Flexible.

29. While working, do you:

    E   *a.* Respond positively to interruptions.

    I   *b.* Object to or ignore interruptions.

30. Is your learning style:

    S   *a.* Step-by-step, and methodical.

    N   *b.* According to overall concept, guided by inspiration.

4

31. In practice, which do you value more:

   T *a.* Truth.

   F *b.* Harmony.

32. Do you tend to:

   J *a.* Finish important matters ahead of time.

   P *b.* Postpone important matters until the last minute.

Now go back and count up all the letters corresponding to your selection.

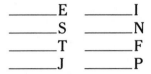

EXTRAVERTED VERSUS INTROVERTED

If you selected more (E) responses, then you are extraverted. You are energized by talking, socializing, and working with people or exploring the outside world.

If you selected more (I) responses, then you are introverted. You are energized by working quietly alone, reading, meditating, or participating in activities which involve few other people.

SENSING VERSUS INTUITION

If you selected more (S) responses, then you are most concerned with facts, experience, details, and reality. You are a sensing type.

If you selected more (N) responses, then you are most interested in possibilities, visions, and the future. You are intuitive.

THINKING VERSUS FEELING

If you selected more (T) responses, then you tend to see things impersonally and objectively. You are a thinking type.

If you selected more (F) responses, then you tend to judge situations according to what's good for people and what promotes harmony. You are a feeling type.

JUDGING VERSUS PERCEIVING

If you selected more (J) responses, then you prefer closure, deadlines, and conclusions. You are a judging type.

If you selected more (P) responses, then you prefer flexibility, open options, and artificial deadlines. You are a perceiving type.

KEEPING IN TOUCH WITH TYPE

Even this short survey can help you make the most of the different personality styles in your company or department. Take a minute to think how you might type the imaginary employees discussed thus far. Can you guess whether they fit the types covered in the Psychological Type Survey? Next, consider how colleagues and co-workers in your group might fit into these types. For a greater understanding of the effects of personality types on work habits and skills, many managers have turned to the now extensive publications based on *Gifts Differing* by Myers and Briggs. A short workshop on personality types can sometimes energize a whole working group.

Naturally, the ideal working group includes all type combinations. Each type contributes to the productivity of the group. For example, introverts reflect on how things are going, intuitive types help with long-range planning, feeling types are conscious of customers' and co-workers' needs, perceiving types easily adapt to changes. Sensing types keep their eyes on the bottom line, thinking types evaluate objectively, and judging types don't let us forget about deadlines.

Unfortunately, companies or departments dominated by the same types don't do very well when faced with changes or new problems. Everyone tends to see things very much alike. There's no one around to answer the question "Where did we go wrong?"

As a good manager you can make your employees aware of their different types and teach them to understand and complement each other better in completing departmental tasks and in developing new approaches to problem solving. Stressing the importance of productivity and meeting deadlines, you can encourage them to draw on the strengths of other members of the team. Once you have the tasks and the degree of cooperation expected in focus, then the differences in personality type become positive rather than negative issues.

> ### What's Your Type?
>
> Give the personality type test to your staff at the next staff meeting. Openly discuss everyone's results, as well as your own.

When you introduce a new project at a meeting, solicit ideas and approaches from employees on the basis of their personality characteristics (E, I, S, N, T, F, J, P). Here's an example of this technique: "Jose, because you are particularly sensitive to customers' feelings, how do you think they will react to this new advertising campaign?" and "Sarah, because you are so deadline oriented, project how long it will take to complete this project?" and "Jan, since you are always open to new ideas, what do you see as an alternative campaign?"

CREATE A TEAM OF TYPES

Knowing your own type and the types of your workers and then working to the best advantage of each will prove to be a very valuable strategy when you need to unite the team in any group effort. Once you have camaraderie established on the basis of a true appreciation of team members' skills, members will be more likely to feel motivated toward achieving a common goal. Keep the group united by giving occasional reminders of the energy generated from personality-type differences.

Chapter Checkpoints

✓ Be sensitive to the different psychological types of the staff.

✓ Solicit ideas and approaches from employees.

✓ Know your own psychological type—weaknesses and strengths.

✓ Encourage appreciation of differences in a group—focus on the energy generated by diversity.

5 | Preparing the New Employee

This chapter will help you to:

- Consider how to make staff changes painless.
- Determine how to ease the departure of a worker.
- Identify ways to organize the arrival of a new worker.

New employees join departments or companies whenever there are increased workloads, retirements, transfers, terminations, reorganizations, or expansions.

As in a social setting, people have different reactions toward new arrivals. Some will regard the newcomer as a threat. Others will enjoy the prospect of working with a new colleague and will extend a warm welcome. Many will be polite but suspicious.

If you, as the manager, properly prepare the workers for the new arrival, you can allay many fears and suspicions. If possible, make the department part of the selection process.

For example, before you place an ad or contact an employment agency, announce that there is a job position open and cite the necessary qualifications. Ask if anyone on your staff knows an available person with those qualifications and encourage staff members to submit the appropriate résumé. The positive side to this approach is that the employees will like being part of the selection process. However, there might be resentment if one employee's recommendation is selected over another's.

Regardless of the reasons for the change in the department staff, the manager must make the adjustment smooth for everyone. Let's take a look at some situations that illustrate the ways that a new employee might be introduced.

5

After these scenarios, write your suggestions for ways to improve these potentially disastrous setups.

1.   Supervisor Leticia enters the office area with a new employee. She guides him over to the desk that had been set up the day before. Leticia speaks with him privately, hands him a box of supplies, and then leaves the area. The new employee sorts through some papers in his briefcase, then begins to set up his desk. After ten long minutes, he approaches the nearest employee, introduces himself as Rafael, the new corporate tax specialist, and then asks where the men's room is. After he leaves, there is much whispering among the staff, which Leticia notices as she reenters the office area.

2. Production Manager Mohammed calls a brief meeting for the staffs of both the assembly unit and the electronic circuits departments. He opens the meeting with an announcement that Ciro from assembly will now be working in electronics and Marcia from electronics will now be working in assembly. He discusses new work assignments and deadlines for each department. When there are no questions, he adjourns the meeting and watches the silent group retreat to their workstations. Mohammed is puzzled by the response of the departments. He was prepared for a longer meeting because he expected a lot of questions about the transfers from these usually vocal groups.

3. Chief claims adjuster Pat had planned the retirement party for Bessie weeks in advance. She wanted it to be very special because Bessie had worked in the claims department since the company had first opened up 23 years ago. Bessie was loved and respected by everyone in the company and she would be sorely missed. Pat had decided to include Maurice, Bessie's replacement, because he would need to quickly establish a relationship with the same people who would be at the party. She was disappointed to see the cordial but cool reception that Maurice was getting. Often she would see him standing by himself, smiling stiffly. She had tried to work him into some groups that were standing around, but the groups would break apart as soon as she walked away. It was as awkward for Pat as it was for Maurice. ■

In each scenario, the managers made mistakes. In the spaces below, identify the mistakes and write ways in which you would have handled the same situations.

1. _____
_____
_____
_____
_____
_____

2. _____
_____
_____
_____
_____
_____

3. _____

_____

_____

_____

_____

_____

CHECK YOUR TECHNIQUE

If you included some of the following techniques you are on the right track to becoming a true motivator.

Solution 1.   Leticia should have told the staff that corporate tax cases were becoming a function of their department and that an additional person—a specialist in corporate tax—was needed. When Rafael was hired, she should have immediately taken him on a tour of the premises and introduced him to everyone. The day before he started, she should have met with the staff and explained why she hired Rafael. She should have told them that because of his specialization, the entire department would be able to absorb the new work efficiently. She could then have asked if anyone would help him out the first few days by introducing him to and assisting him in learning policies and procedures. On Rafael's first day, a brief, informal gathering should have been held so that the staff could officially welcome him.

In this way, there would have been no mystery about the new employee's role, motives, or identity.

Solution 2.   Mohammed dropped a bombshell on two departments and then was surprised because no one asked questions. Everyone saw the transfers as punitive because they had heard rumors that Ciro and Marcia were having difficulties in their respective departments. Even though the truth was that they both had been warned about lack of productivity and personality conflicts, for everyone concerned it was better to present the transfers as moves for positive reasons.

By mentioning the transfers at the beginning of the meeting, Mohammed gave this news primary importance but with no explanation. Mohammed could have put everyone at ease and even encouraged an open discussion by announcing the transfers at the end of the meeting as a bit of good news. He could have said that Ciro had a background in electronics circuits and wanted to get back into that line of work. He could have mentioned that Marcia needed a break after several years of work in the assembly unit and would benefit from practical experience to augment her studies in electronics.

Mohammed would have been seen as a manager willing to help employees find their niche. Marcia and Ciro would not be ostracized because they were on their way out. The other employees would be reassured that management tried to find a solution that benefited rather than punished employees.

Solution 3.   Pat made a mistake by inviting Maurice. The party was a bittersweet occasion for Bessie. She is ending a significant phase in her life and will no longer be a part of the daily lives of her co-workers. She deserved an entire celebration devoted to her.

Maurice will have a difficult enough time trying to take Bessie's place. Meeting people under those circumstances only reminds people that Bessie will soon be gone and Maurice will be replacing her. Maurice deserves a better beginning for his new career.

Instead of hiring one person to do Bessie's work, Pat should redistribute the workload among all of the staff. In this way no one person will be taking Bessie's place. Maurice should then be introduced to the staff as a new employee who will be helping to absorb some of Bessie's and the other's tasks.

Maurice should have his own introductory gathering after Bessie leaves. With the redistribution of Bessie's work, there will be less opportunity to compare Maurice's ability with hers. It will also enable Maurice to establish his own identity without direct association with Bessie's retirement. His colleagues will be less likely to judge him and welcome him to share the workload.

INTRODUCTIONS *WORK*

Although Leticia, Mohammed, and Pat made management mistakes, their efforts were admirable because they did attempt to ease in a new employee. With more practice, they will likely develop the expertise needed to make transition much easier.

Changes are always stressful when the circumstances are not clearly understood by everyone involved. It is the responsibility of the manager to prepare the staff by making the proper arrangements before changes occur. Make sure that time is set aside to introduce new workers, to say good-bye to old workers, and to adjust to departmental changes. Otherwise, more time may be lost later when dealing with problems resulting from misinformation.

Write in the space provided the positive steps taken by each manager.

1. Leticia's positive efforts were to:

_____

_____

_____

2. Mohammed's positive efforts were to:

_____

_____

_____

3. Pat's positive efforts were to:

_____

_____

_____

CHECK YOUR ANALYSIS

1. Leticia had Rafael's physical surroundings set up for him. She provided him with a desk and supplies and then gave him some time to get acquainted on his own. Sometimes that works; often it doesn't, but at least he wasn't sitting at an empty desk with absolutely nothing to do. Presumably, when she returned to the office, she planned to make introductions.
2. Calling a meeting to discuss the transfers was a good move for Mohammed to make. Allowing extra time for discussion was an important and positive step, although the way in which he made the announcement dampened anyone's desire to discuss it openly.
3. Organizing a retirement party was a very thoughtful gesture for Pat to make. Efforts like that go a long way in improving employee relations. Pat's invitation to Maurice was also very thoughtful, though misguided.

Suggestion

Invite Everyone to Join the Welcome Wagon

When a new employee joins a department, the manager must help the other employees to adjust. Prepare them before the new worker arrives, ask for one person to volunteer as a buddy for a few days, hold an informal, introductory gathering, and make sure that everyone's roles are clearly defined.

5

Chapter Checkpoints

✓ Prepare employees in advance for a new member's arrival.

✓ If possible, involve other department members in a job search for a new employee.

✓ Hold an informal, introductory gathering for each new employee.

✓ Help problem employees find their niches by offering departmental transfers.

✓ Dispel notions that transfers are punitive—present them as fresh starts and opportunities for career growth.

6 | Preparing the New Supervisor

This chapter will help you to:

- Ease the entry of a new supervisor.
- Consider the perspectives of the workers when dealing with a new supervisor.
- Evaluate strategies for a successful transition.

New supervisors arrive for much the same reasons any new employee joins a company: expansion, increased workload, retirement, transfer, termination, resignation of the former supervisor, or company reorganization. The response of the staff largely depends on the overtures made by the new supervisor. Often, staff members fear that their jobs are in jeopardy if they cannot get along with the new boss. Most employees remain in a holding pattern until they get a feel for the new manager's style.

As in the case of a new employee, the manager bears most of the responsibility for making the adjustment a smooth one for everyone.

Let's take a look at a scenario that illustrates one way in which a new supervisor might handle the introduction to a new department. After the scenario, write your suggestions for ways to improve this shaky beginning.

Day One

Glenda was really excited about the challenge of her new assignment. She was not the least bit concerned that she was the third person hired to shape up a department that had consistently lagged in productivity behind every other department in the firm. The morale of the department was notoriously low, and the workers were known for their unproductive work habits.

Arriving thirty minutes early, Glenda greeted staff members as they arrived. She stayed in the reception area, shook hands with everybody, and welcomed each one warmly.

Glenda called a meeting. She enumerated the problems within the department, and then outlined her strategies for solving the problems. She assigned a role for each worker and then asked for everyone's complete cooperation.

Glenda ended the meeting with a cheery, ''Let's not waste any more time, okay? Everybody, off to work we go!'' The group retreated to the office area and milled about quietly discussing the meeting. When Glenda saw that the staff had mobilized to chat rather than work, she tried to circulate in each group to determine the problem. What she heard was a mixture of complaints, excuses, accusations, insincere praise for her intentions, skepticism, and boasting. No one seemed ready to join her team. ■

Glenda made some mistakes, but she was on the right track. In the space below, list the positives and negatives of Glenda's approach:

Positives: _____

_____

_____

_____

Negatives: _____

_____

_____

_____

How would you improve Glenda's chances of success with her new team?

_____

_____

_____

_____

_____

_____

Here are some possible responses. On the positive side:

1. Glenda's personal, warm greeting on her first day was an affirming act.
2. Calling a meeting to outline her intentions was a good way to involve everyone in the new leadership plan.
3. Assigning tasks openly was an efficient way to avoid accusations of uneven work distribution.
4. Joining the small gatherings of workers after her introduction demonstrated her commitment. Her willingness to discuss problems shows her group that Glenda is concerned and willing to listen.

On the negative side:

1. Prior to the first official meeting, it would have been better not only to greet, but to have a brief chat with each worker at his or her work station.

6

2. Rather than enumerating the problems within the department at the meeting, it would have been better to emphasize departmental strengths and leave the negatives for individual discussions.
3. Glenda should have asked for the employees' input regarding work assignments. Individual preferences may prove to be critical when trying to break a cycle of low productivity.
4. Her remark, "Let's not waste any more time," probably offended some workers because it implies that they have not been working or that meetings are a waste of time.

If Glenda had waited a few days before calling her first meeting, she may have had more insight about the group's problems. Her first few days should have been spent observing patterns and work habits. She also should have met with the workers individually to get their perspectives on the problems within the department.

Glenda should have met with the leader within the group and then invited him or her to join forces to improve their team. The departmental meeting would then be less formal and provide an opportunity to reiterate her optimism for the department based on her observations. The meeting would have become a morale boosting celebration, which is precisely what Glenda needs to begin her reform movement.

Suggestion ————————————————

Let's Do Lunch

If the company doesn't organize a formal introductory gathering for you, organize your own informal gathering of the staff you now supervise. Invest in a casual get-acquainted luncheon at a local, favorite dining spot (ask for recommendations from your new staff) or simply provide a light snack for everyone to share around 3:30. The break will be welcome and will be a productive way to get everyone involved in the transition.

HURRY UP, BUT GO SLOWLY

Whenever a new manager takes over an area, many overdue changes (perhaps accepted for years) become obvious. In an effort to excel and demonstrate competence, managers often move too quickly to make these improvements, alienating staff members rather than uniting them behind the new manager. Gradual changes, lengthy discreet observations of interaction, and acknowledgments of past performances are worthwhile investments of time.

Managers must be patient and understanding about the difficult adjustments that employees must make in order to fit in with the new plans. The period of adjustment may last six months or even longer. The wait is worthwhile if you finally build a solid, productive team.

6

Chapter Checkpoints

✓ Clearly outline intended changes in new departments.

✓ Assign tasks openly.

✓ Demonstrate sincere concern and a willingness to listen to employees.

✓ Emphasize departmental strengths at meetings.

✓ Take time to observe patterns and work habits in a new department.

✓ Implement changes gradually.

7 | Resolving Conflicts

This chapter will help you to:

- Identify typical inter- or intradepartmental disputes.
- Consider problem solving techniques.
- Evaluate long- and short-term solutions.

Name one completely harmonious work environment and chances are that you've named a one-person company. When co-workers spend a lot of time together, conflicts are natural.

In a work situation the manager must evaluate each conflict much like a parent and determine the severity of the rift. The manager must search for motivation, cause, and point of origin. You must listen to all sides—especially those not directly involved—in order to get a more objective perspective. Finding a resolution may be difficult and might not always be fair to everyone. If a manager mistakenly waits for things to blow over, the problems will fester and become unsolvable.

The following illustrations have three possible solutions. Select the one that you feel best solves the problem.

1. Dispute at the Drill Press

Foreman Wilfredo hears a loud argument erupt between co-workers, John and Brian. They are standing next to a drill press that appears to be malfunctioning, and it looks as if they are about to become physically violent. As a crowd gathers, Wilfredo debates how to react to the confrontation. ■

Solution A.   Wilfredo asks two of the biggest workers to separate John and Brian. He announces they will lose a half-day's wages and sends them home. When John and Brian return the next day, Wilfredo tells them that fights will

not be tolerated regardless of the cause and the next one will result in termination.

Solution B. Wilfredo observes the argument to identify the aggressor and the problem. He calmly disperses the crowd and escorts the aggressor, John, to his office. He asks John to calm down and explain the problem. John says that he has told Brian many times before that the press must not be turned on before checking that the knobs are all in the down position. John operates the drill press after Brian and usually finds the press improperly set and the area around it strewn with debris.

Brian later explains to Wilfredo that John is exaggerating the condition of the press and the area around it. Brian also finds the area messy and does not feel responsible for cleaning up after another worker. He admits that the malfunction of the drill press is his fault, and he promises to be more careful.

Wilfredo posts a sign for all employees to read. The sign says each worker is fully responsible for the condition of the equipment and the surrounding area. Failure to comply with this maintenance rule may result in suspension or termination.

Solution C. Wilfredo retreats to his office and calls out through the intercom for John and Brian to report immediately to his office. He asks them to sit down and explain the problem. After listening to both sides, he sends them back to work. He then calls in two other reliable witnesses to corroborate or refute each version.

After comparing all four versions, Wilfredo decides to penalize Brian by docking his pay a half-day's wages and charging him for any costs incurred repairing the drill press.

2. Faculty Feud

Keesha and Robert have worked together in the English department for about three semesters. They frequently have lunch together and occasionally socialize after work.

The department chairperson, Molly, is surprised to hear that Keesha has been complaining to her students about Robert. She told them to avoid taking a course with him because he does not prepare students adequately for the more advanced English courses.

Molly observes Keesha and Robert for a few days and notices that they are barely civil to each other. Soon after, she enters the faculty workroom and finds the two of them silently grading papers. She contemplates a solution. ■

Solution A. Molly silently leaves the room. She hopes that if Keesha and Robert are alone, they will work out their problems together. Molly feels that their dispute is of a personal nature and it would be intrusive to even raise the issue.

Solution B. Molly enters the room and sits down between them. She tells them there seems to be a problem that is affecting them at work. If it is a work-related problem, she tells them, she wants to resolve it immediately so that they can continue their exemplary performances in the classroom. She asks, "What can I do to help?"

7

When neither speaks up, she assumes the problem is personal, so she rises to leave. She reiterates that they are both valuable instructors and she hopes that they can resume their former professional relationship. She warns them that if the problem is personal, they had better "leave it at home."

Solution C.   Molly stands in the doorway and asks Keesha to come to her office in an hour. When Keesha arrives, all Molly does is ask what is going on and Keesha tearfully admits that her relationship with Robert has become more than platonic. Although both Keesha and Robert knew the pitfalls of an office romance, they became romantically involved and it did not work out. She claims that Robert ended the relationship, and now she is bitter.

When Molly summons Robert to her office the next day, he is reluctant to discuss something so personal with his supervisor. He admits that it was a mistake to get involved with a co-worker and for that reason decided to end it. Actually, he is already involved with someone else. He apologizes to Molly for allowing his personal life to interfere with his work. He says he is uncomfortable discussing it and would like to leave unless there is something work-related that she wants to discuss.

Molly allows him to go but requests that he speak with Keesha. She asks him to try to establish a civil relationship with Keesha because it is unfair to sever ties with a colleague when students and work are so frequently shared.

3. Clash at the Check Cashing Counter

Janice slowly and methodically counts out a customer's cash. At the next bank window, Chung rapidly cashes checks and takes deposits. For every four customers that Chung serves, Janice only handles one. Her customers don't complain, but several are seen changing from her line to Chung's.

At one point, Chung tells the customers, "If you don't want to be here all day, you'd better get in my line." Janice mumbles under her breath but continues to work at a slow pace. She remains polite to her customers but frequently glares over at Chung who seems to enjoy taunting her.

▮ Suggestion ──────────────────────────────────

Any Suggestions?

Having a suggestion box is an effective device for spotting problems before they become major conflicts. Often, employees are unwilling to openly report minor problems and hope that they will go away in time. Unfortunately, minor problems, if unattended, can become big conflicts that involve many people and disrupt the workplace.

A simple solution is to install a suggestion box in an isolated area where employees can feel comfortable depositing an anonymous comment or suggestion. Managers will be enlightened, educated, and well-informed about inter/intraoffice politics. Employee input goes a long way toward avoiding potential problems.

When Chung has no customers, she watches Janice and laughs at her when she miscounts or drops change. Finally, Janice runs crying from her counter and tells the manager, Toya, that she cannot take the pressure. She leaves the bank before Toya decides how to handle the situation. ▪

Solution A.   Toya speaks with three other employees who regularly work with both Chung and Janice. Then she calls Janice at home. She tells her that she is a valuable employee and many customers appreciate her accuracy and courtesy. Toya promises to transfer Chung to another area where she will have minimal contact with her.

Toya speaks directly to Chung. She tells her that although her speed is appreciated by some, there are other customers who prefer Janice's approach. She admonishes her for such childish teasing. Toya asks Chung if she would like to work at the drive-in window, where speed is a priority for customers, or at the payroll check cashing window. She tells her that remaining at her present position is not an option and she must stay as far away from Janice as possible.

Solution B.   Toya waits for Janice to come back to work the next day, when she is calmer. Toya tells her she will not dock her for leaving two hours early. She calls Chung over and tells them to shake hands. She advises them to go out to lunch together so that they may discuss their differences and work them out.

Solution C.   Toya holds a staff meeting to discuss personality conflicts and productivity fluctuations on the job. She addresses the issues of accuracy versus speed, customers' needs, and employee interaction. She does not openly discuss Chung and Janice's problem but everyone knows their dispute is what precipitated the meeting.

Toya gently but firmly reminds the staff to respect each other and concentrate on the customers. She tells them that open conflicts will not be tolerated and that courtesy toward customers and colleagues is a must in order to keep their jobs.

BEST SOLUTIONS

All of the solutions are acceptable. However, if you selected B for 1, B for 2, and A for 3, you picked the three best solutions.

1.   Solution B is best. By escorting the aggressor, John, away from the scene, Wilfredo effectively diffused the anger. By listening to John's version, he allowed him to vent his frustration and to feel that his viewpoint was important.

Because Wilfredo listened to all sides he was able to make an informed decision. Brian was definitely at fault. But it was also necessary to acknowledge his complaint about other workers.

The posted sign gives Brian some small satisfaction that the foreman believed that he was not the only one to leave work areas messy. The sign also assuages John's feelings by giving notice to all workers that they must be responsible for equipment and work areas.

Solution C is also fair but it does not leave any favorable opening for Brian. If no one corroborated Brian's claim that others are occasionally sloppy, the penalties cited for Brian would be the best.

2.   Solution B does not put Robert and Keesha in the embarrassing position of having to discuss their personal lives. Molly is making herself available to them if they want to confide in her. She is letting

them know that their estrangement is obvious and may affect them professionally.

By confronting them together and then leaving them alone, Molly has given Robert and Keesha an opportunity to work things out without getting too involved herself. This approach is preferable to the approach in solution C where Molly's involvement is too personal. By confronting Robert directly about personal matters, his relationship with Keesha may be worsened. He feels resentful that Keesha has revealed so much to Molly and will probably blame her for any professional problems that may result.

3. Number 3 is best solved by solution A. Toya investigates the situation and takes appropriate action. She saves two good employees by acknowledging their distinctive abilities and offers Chung a choice which makes her a part of the solution. She reassures Janice by removing the pressure of Chung's scrutiny and ridicule.

Solution C would have been the better choice if Toya had not let things get to the crisis stage. Had she been aware of Chung's behavior earlier, the staff meeting would have effectively limited Chung's harassment.

In solution B the manager is deflecting the problem rather than solving it.

MOVE TOWARD RESOLUTION

When an otherwise motivated staff begins to show signs of strain by bickering, complaining, and aggression, it is time to evaluate the causes and propose the best solution.

1. The manager must take time to observe those involved.

2. Speak with staff members individually to hear different perspectives.

3. Diffuse anger by separating warring employees.

4. Offer choices to the offending worker.

5. Reassure and support the injured worker.

When resolving conflicts, managers must remember to remain calm. It's easy to get swept up in the emotions of the moment, but once that happens, it's difficult to deal with the situation objectively.

If you determine that the underlying cause of conflict is undue pressure to meet deadlines or quotas, make adjustments in schedules where you can. Negotiate for more time, if possible. If intradepartmental competition is fueling conflict, openly discuss strategies to reduce friction.

Personal problems should be kept out of the workplace. Guide employees toward more appropriate ways of resolving problems that impact on the working environment. Remember that most employees' personal crises pass into history—just make sure they do *quickly*.

7

Chapter Checkpoints

✓ Listen to all sides of any worker dispute.

✓ Never allow employee problems to fester.

✓ Offer choices, reassurance, and support to parties involved in a dispute.

8 | Motivational Techniques

This chapter will help you to:

- Develop necessary observational skills.
- Identify individual and group needs and goals.
- Implement practices to meet group needs and goals.

Managers can motivate workers by providing a work environment that satisfies workers' inner needs while achieving organizational objectives that will benefit everyone.

In order to determine these needs, managers must listen and observe. When the climate of the workplace changes, it is critical to determine causes and reorient the staff. By listening and observing, you will be able to assess the damage, isolate the offenders, and plan effective strategies.

Proper timing and technique will make your efforts successful. Train yourself to be sensitive to changes, needs, and interaction. This chapter will help you develop observational skills and take action to motivate everyone in your group. A motivated group is a productive group.

Employee needs vary, of course, but most require the following items:

1. Security.
2. Desirable type of work.
3. Desirable company.
4. Friendly co-workers.
5. Good supervisor.
6. Advancement.
7. Recognition.

8. Good working conditions.
9. Good benefits.
10. Good pay.

Although at times it may seem an overwhelming task to meet these needs, there are managerial techniques you can implement that will help you achieve this goal.

Effective Management Techniques

1. Keep employees informed.
2. Treat everyone as professionals.
3. Periodically reorganize work flow.
4. Examine expectations, both yours and theirs.
5. Solicit opinions.
6. Make no value judgments.

7. Provide timely follow-through.

8. Be generous and open with praise.

9. Encourage career growth.

10. Listen, understand, and respect.

1. Make a list of your career goals at ages 18, 25, 35, 45, 55.

Age	Goals
18	
25	
35	
45	
55	

2. Check off the goals that were met.

3. Circle the goals that were met because of the support, guidance, or influence of a supervisor, mentor, or colleague. Write down their names and titles, if you can remember them.

4. List the perceived goals of your staff (use additional paper if necessary).

Employee	Goals
1.	
2.	
3.	
4.	
5.	
6.	
7.	
8.	
9.	
10.	

5. Circle those goals that you can help your employees to achieve.

8

SUBTLETY AND SINCERITY = SUCCESS

At this point, you probably feel confident about your ability to motivate your staff. If, so far, you have applied all of the techniques discussed in this book, you must be a terrific motivator, right? So why do you continue reading? It may be because the techniques do not work all the time, and you are wondering why.

A common mistake managers make is to underestimate how well the staff knows them, and their expectations. Your role is to observe each worker and plan individual strategies to maximize productivity by elevating and maintaining a high level of motivation. It takes time, but a good manager gets to know many workers fairly well. Imagine how easy it is, then, for an employee to scrutinize only *one* person—*you*. Any changes in your mood, behavior, and approach are rapidly detected by the staff.

If employees are fully aware of the strategies being implemented to motivate them and increase their productivity, they may resent this manipulation and resist your efforts. The key to successful motivation is to implement techniques in a subtle way. Efforts must seem spontaneous and sincere.

Two scenarios that illustrate some subtle and not-so-subtle ways of applying morale-boosting techniques follow:

1. Library Lament

Head librarian, Greg, overhears staff worker, Marguerite, complaining to a co-worker:

"I'm just as qualified as anyone else to run this library. But all I do is check out books—and I am going out of my mind! Greg doesn't seem to know any more than I do, and yet he gets a title and more money. If only he would ask me to take over next time he is out, then you would all see how well I could run this place!" ■

Solution A.   Greg waits about an hour and then he approaches Marguerite to ask her to run the library for him next week when he is at a conference.

Solution A may be misperceived as Greg's attempt to set Marguerite up to fail. It is obvious that Greg is only responding to what he overheard. It certainly wouldn't appear to be a sincere effort to provide Marguerite with an opportunity to apply her skills.

Solution B.   Greg waits until the next morning to approach Marguerite. As soon as she arrives, he calls her into his office. "Marguerite, I was wondering if you could help me out. I have about four pending projects that I've been neglecting because I'm overloaded. I'd like to give you one of them. I know you can handle it, and I would really appreciate your help."

Solution B is safer because Marguerite would not suspect Greg's offer to be the result of overhearing her complaint, and would not need to wonder if it was just a coincidence. She will be flattered to be chosen to help him, and grateful that her ability has been recognized. She will probably work very hard to show everyone how capable she is.

2. Medical Malcontents

At the biannual staff meeting, the last agenda item deals with patient service reviews. The hospital director, Raymond, dreads this item because it means dealing with negative issues and criticism. Patient feedback is often hard on the nursing staff. The recent wage and hiring freeze makes most of the nursing staff feel overworked and unappreciated.

Raymond begins by reassuring the nurses. He tells them that he is aware of how hard they are working, and that although the reviews are mandatory, the negative nature of the comments is a reflection of societal trends and should not be taken personally.

Even with this soothing introduction, the nurses become angry and defensive. They begin blaming each other, supervisory staff, support staff, and the lack of staff. Raymond loses control of the group and ends up adjourning the meeting. ■

Solution A.   Raymond issues an urgent memo notifying the staff of the formation of a committee to be made up of representatives from each department. It will be headed by a representative of the nursing staff, and will examine ways to improve relations between staff and management. It will also be responsible for distributing and evaluating patient service reviews.

The idea of forming a committee is sound. The responsibilities of this particular committee are relevant and necessary. The problem with this response is that the timing is wrong. Raymond should have issued the announcement about the committee prior to the meeting—not as a result.

On the heels of a demoralizing meeting, the announcement looks just like what it is—a weak effort to mollify the staff. The group may not take the committee seriously; it may also change the mission of the committee into a complaint forum.

Raymond is better off announcing the formation of this committee along with some other news in the monthly newsletter. It will be a welcome, better thought-out, secondary response to the workers' expressions of unhappiness. It should follow the response discussed in solution B.

Solution B.   Raymond does not adjourn the meeting. He calls for a short break and orders refreshments. When everyone returns from the break, he asks Sheila, the head of the nursing staff, to join him at the front of the room. He then asks the workers to present their concerns to Sheila, who will note them and present them to management for consideration. He hopes that if they are dealing directly with their immediate supervisor, they will feel less antagonistic.

After giving everyone a chance to air their complaints, he promises to give his immediate attention to the written list. He thanks them for their valuable input and adjourns the meeting on an optimistic note.

A few days later, Raymond submits a rough draft of an employee survey for everyone's review. He announces that, effective immediately, the survey will be distributed biannually to all employees. The survey is an anonymous questionnaire about working conditions at the hospital.

At this point, the formation of the abovementioned committee would be ideal. The committee will collate the surveys and the patient service reviews, and make recommendations to management for improvements.

Raymond is responding in a timely manner to the workers' needs. He is listening to their concerns and recognizing and valuing their abilities by requesting their input and forming a committee. He may not be able to meet all of their demands, but his sincerity and willingness to listen will satisfy most of them.

Suggestion

Let's Get It Together

Form a committee, publish a company newsletter, and distribute surveys just like the ones discussed in Solution B for Raymond's situation. Include a question on the survey that asks for individual goals. Share the information and openly discuss the individual goals at the next staff meeting. See how many goals match the ones you noted in the career goals worksheet.

TUNE-IN AND TURN-ON TECHNIQUES

If you are completely in tune with your workers, you will notice symptoms of discontent. Your observations will help you determine when and how to handle problems. The technique you choose should always be sincere and be responsive to the demoralizing factor involved:

1. Observe your workers.
2. Analyze their needs.
3. Respond in a timely manner.
4. Tailor your motivational techniques to meet the needs of the individual.
5. Be sincere.

Chapter Checkpoints

✓ Implement management techniques in a subtle way.

✓ Make efforts seem spontaneous and sincere.

✓ Respond in a timely manner to workers' needs.

✓ Recognize and value workers' abilities.

✓ Help your employees meet their goals.

CHAPTER

9 | Motivational Maintenance

This chapter will help you to:

- Evaluate the working environment.
- Consider ways to improve the physical workspace.
- Identify and implement motivational maintenance techniques.

The climate in your department has now begun moving toward the comfort zone of supportive productivity. This chapter addresses additional strategies to be implemented to maintain this higher level of motivation.

It's okay to relax within this comfortably motivated environment, but don't relax so much that warning signs go unheeded. Almost overnight, the comfort zone can change into a danger zone and you are back to the beginning.

Take a moment to look around your work environment, then answer the questions below:

1. Are the work areas too close or too far from each other?
2. Are there sufficient doorways leading to other offices or departments?
3. Are there common areas and lounges for employees?
4. Is there music playing in offices or common areas?
5. When was the last time the walls were painted?
6. Are there plants, pictures, and/or bulletin boards in common areas?
7. What is the flooring of the office and common area—rugs? tile?
8. Is the office furniture practical, comfortable, and attractive?
9. Are there windows? If so, are there blinds and/or draperies?
10. Do you publish a company newsletter?

11. Are there employees on the staff of the newsletter?

12. Is a worker opinion survey regularly distributed?

Some of these questions may not apply to your particular work situation. Wherever practical, try implementing changes based on your answers. The positive effects of even small alterations can be amazing.

CONVENIENCE OF COMMUNICATION

How easy is it for workers to communicate with each other, other departments, or people in management? There may be several methods of communication available, but if they are inconvenient, employees won't bother. Open communication is the key to avoiding misinformation, misunderstandings, and misperceptions.

Workers are often stimulated by the exchange of new ideas and new methods. They energize each other. Open areas for communication will satisfy this need for social interaction.

Whenever and wherever possible, managers should make communication convenient.

IS YOUR AREA OVERSTIMULATED?

How do loud noises, bright colors, and uncomfortable furniture affect your productivity and mood? Many studies have been done on the effects of color in classrooms, hospitals, shopping malls, and offices. Soothing colors such as light blues, greens, and pinks have positive effects. Calm, low-volume music has a relaxing effect. Lighting has a strong influence depending on the type of work being done.

Suggestion

Where's the Party?

Schedule an annual picnic or a holiday party. Invite the entire company. If the event is not financially feasible, then ask for refreshment and supply contributions. Have each department choose a representative to help organize the festivities. Include everyone from maintenance to management.

9

REDECORATE

Not only is it vital to surround your workers with a pleasant and stimulating environment, but it is equally important to alter the look and feel of the environment from time to time. Monotonous surroundings have a strong negative influence on workers, particularly if the nature of their work is monotonous.

Change is good if it is not too extreme or sudden. Alert the workers to the decorating plans and solicit their input. Support the workers' need to personalize their areas with mementos, photos, and artwork. Give them a sense of proprietary involvement in their work environment.

REDISTRIBUTE AND RENEW

Do you have a department staffed by specialists? Not only do monotonous surroundings slow down production, but imagine the long-term effects of routine work performed by rote. The reassignment of work projects to other staff members stimulates healthy competition. With proper guidance and support, most workers will welcome an opportunity to stretch. The entire group will have the opportunity to refresh its approach. Individuals will begin to seek new projects that are not normally within their domain. Reassigning projects periodically is a good way for managers to encourage career growth while stimulating productivity.

REFRESH—INSIDE AND OUT

It should be your mission as a manager to keep your team stimulated. Individual social, intellectual, and professional needs should always be considered. By providing a pleasant working environment with opportunities for a healthy exchange of ideas—personal as well as professional, you ensure that many important social needs are met. By discussing and reassigning work in formal and informal settings, you help to meet many professional growth needs.

With this larger, external effort, maintaining a high level of motivation should be simply a matter of addressing individual problems as they arise.

9

Chapter Checkpoints

✓ Make communication between workers and departments convenient.

✓ Provide a pleasant and stimulating work environment.

✓ Support workers' needs to personalize their work areas.

✓ Encourage and provide opportunities for career growth.

Post-Test

Now that you have been armed with new ideas, strategies, and techniques, it's time to check your own motivational level again. Next to each of the 15 statements below, give yourself 1, 2, 3, or 4 points depending on the following scale: (1) Always; (2) Usually; (3) Sometimes; (4) Never.

_____	**1.** I wake up wishing it were Friday.
_____	**2.** I avoid the company of co-workers.
_____	**3.** I eat lunch with people I don't work with.
_____	**4.** I prefer limited, unspecified tasks.
_____	**5.** The day usually goes slowly for me.
_____	**6.** I feel most meetings are a waste of time.
_____	**7.** I know very little about my workers' personal lives.
_____	**8.** My workers know very little about my private life.
_____	**9.** Interoffice gossip is interesting to me.
_____	**10.** I feel overworked, underpaid, and unappreciated.
_____	**11.** My staff feels overworked, underpaid, and unappreciated.
_____	**12.** I look in the classified section for better job possibilities.
_____	**13.** My family knows very little about my job and staff.
_____	**14.** I feel I could do a much better job at work.
_____	**15.** I am unsure of my supervisor's opinion of me.

Add up the points. Total = _____

If you scored between 15 and 30 points, you still have many doubts and insecurities which will prevent you from motivating your staff.

If you scored between 31 and 50 points, then you made a start to improving your level of motivation. Evaluate your weak areas and go back to the appropriate chapters and begin applying some of the techniques suggested.

If you scored between 51 and 60 points, congratulations and good luck in your mission to feel and instill *motivation at work*!

THE BUSINESS SKILLS EXPRESS SERIES

This growing series of books addresses a broad range of key business skills and topics to meet the needs of employees, human resource departments, and training consultants.

To obtain information about these and other Business Skills Express books, please call Business One IRWIN toll free at: 1-800-634-3966.

Effective Performance Management	ISBN	1-55623-867-3
Hiring the Best	ISBN	1-55623-865-7
Writing that Works	ISBN	1-55623-856-8
Customer Service Excellence	ISBN	1-55623-969-6
Writing for Business Results	ISBN	1-55623-854-1
Powerful Presentation Skills	ISBN	1-55623-870-3
Meetings that Work	ISBN	1-55623-866-5
Effective Teamwork	ISBN	1-55623-880-0
Time Management	ISBN	1-55623-888-6
Assertiveness Skills	ISBN	1-55623-857-6
Motivation at Work	ISBN	1-55623-868-1
Overcoming Anxiety at Work	ISBN	1-55623-869-X
Positive Politics at Work	ISBN	1-55623-879-7
Telephone Skills at Work	ISBN	1-55623-858-4
Managing Conflict at Work	ISBN	1-55623-890-8
The New Supervisor: Skills for Success	ISBN	1-55623-762-6
The *Americans with Disabilities Act*: What Supervisors Need to Know	ISBN	1-55623-889-4